Out o

Written by **Jillian Sullivan**
Illustrated by **Graham O'Neill**

Rigby®

HOUGHTON MIFFLIN HARCOURT

It was hard for Sam and his older brother Paul to believe what happened up in the mountains that day. It was a blue-sky day after a snowy week, and the runs had bumpy, packed powder. The chairlifts had a long line of people waiting, and the brothers were fed up with waiting for rides and then having to dodge all the other people on the runs.

"I'm going higher up the mountain for some fresh powder snow," Paul said. "I'll see you later."

"I'm coming, too," said Sam.

"No, you're not!" said Paul. "It's too steep for you."

"I can do it," protested Sam. "You can't stop me!"

SKI LIFT

OPEN

CLOSED

3

The boys hiked painstakingly for about forty-five minutes up the snowy slopes. They were forced to take small steps, lifting one foot after the other in the deep snow, but gradually, they made their way higher and higher, until they entered an out-of-bounds area. Neither saw the warning signs.

At the top of the climb, the boys looked down on a sparkling pathway that led down to a lake. "All that powder snow just for the two of us," said Paul.

It was steep… steeper than any slope Sam had ever been on before, and the frozen lake looked like a faraway jewel.

"Think you can do it, little brother?" Paul asked.

"Sure!" said Sam, but inside his chest, his heart was pounding with fear.

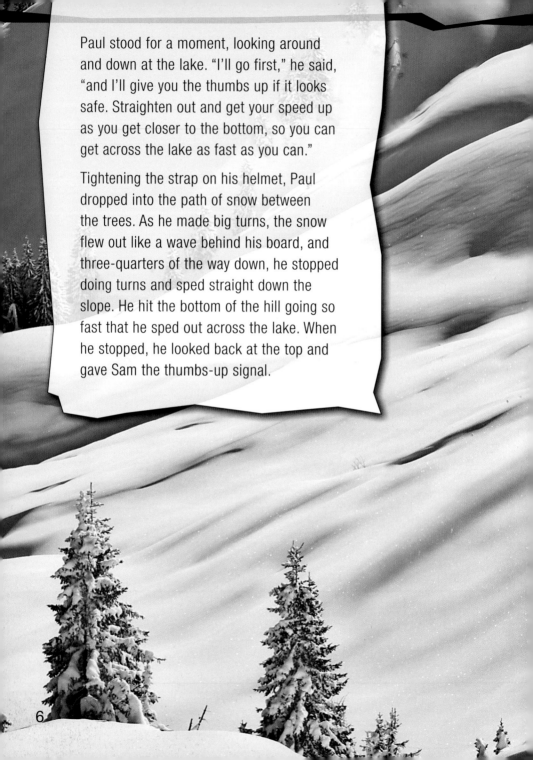

Paul stood for a moment, looking around and down at the lake. "I'll go first," he said, "and I'll give you the thumbs up if it looks safe. Straighten out and get your speed up as you get closer to the bottom, so you can get across the lake as fast as you can."

Tightening the strap on his helmet, Paul dropped into the path of snow between the trees. As he made big turns, the snow flew out like a wave behind his board, and three-quarters of the way down, he stopped doing turns and sped straight down the slope. He hit the bottom of the hill going so fast that he sped out across the lake. When he stopped, he looked back at the top and gave Sam the thumbs-up signal.

Sam took a deep breath of the cold mountain air and edged to the top of the slope on his snowboard as Paul watched from below. Sam had ridden a black diamond run last winter, but that was nothing compared to the height of the run he was facing. He had a burning desire to show his brother he could do it, and his desire beat his fear. He dropped down into the chute of snow and was soon making the big turns on the slope. He knew he had to judge and make every turn just right, or he could hit a tree or the side of a cliff.

Like Paul had done before him, Sam stopped making turns and went straight down the last part. His stomach grew tight with excitement and fear as he raced faster and faster. He felt like a bird swooping in the clean air as he sped toward the frozen lake at the bottom of the hill. The ice spread out in front of him, glinting in the sun.

Straightening his legs, Sam made it from the steep slope onto the frozen lake. From gliding down on soft powder snow, his board whizzed across the ice, catching up to Paul where he stood waiting.

"Hey, you did good! You were awesome!" said Paul. "Come on. Let's get off this lake." Turning around, Paul started walking with his board under his arm.

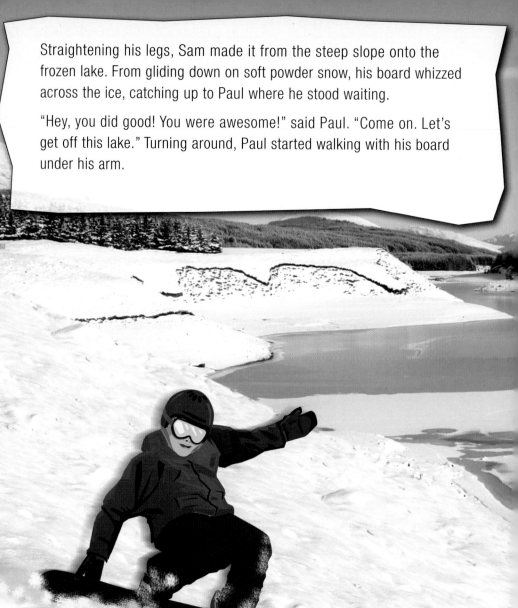

Sam looked back to see once again how high he had been and how steep the slope was. That's when there was a huge boom, and he saw the hillside coming down towards them.

"AVALANCHE!" he screamed.

In one second, he had the board off his feet, and the brothers were running for their lives. Behind them the snow and rocks pounded onto the lake. As they ran, cracks zigzagged in the ice between their legs and opened up in front of them. Sam ran so fast his breath was just a cold ache in his chest.

The cracks on the ice got bigger and bigger, and the brothers could feel the lake moving underneath them as more and more snow thundered onto the ice. By the time they got to the middle of the lake, the cracks in the ice were so wide they could see water. Paul threw his board down on the lake and dived onto it on his stomach.

Sam copied him and, using his arms, 'paddled' his board over the cracking ice. At the edge of the lake, they hauled themselves off their boards and stood up, their chests heaving. They looked in horror at the pile of snow that had come down on the ice where they had just been, and the reality of the situation hit home as they struggled to catch their breath.

It wasn't long before the ski patrol turned up.

"Are you boys okay?" a man asked.

Sam and Paul nodded.

"You've had a lucky escape," said the team leader. "Did you know there was a high risk of avalanche today?"

"No," said Paul.

"Avalanches are common after a big snowfall. Next time you want to come up to these areas, come and talk to us first, and look for the warning signs we put up. That's what we're here for—to help keep you safe."

"We're going up to the top now to be sure no one else got caught," said the man. "Then we'll see you back at headquarters to talk it over."

After the patrol team left, Paul looked at Sam and then out at the cracked lake, which was partially covered with a mass of avalanche snow. "How are you feeling?" he asked.

Sam's hands were wet and icy inside his gloves, and his legs were still shaking like jelly. "Alive," he said.

"Me, too," said Paul.

Narratives

A narrative tells a story through a sequence of events. Narratives can be about imagined or true events.

How to Write a Narrative

≫ Step One

- Make a list of topics. Choose a topic that you know about and that readers will find interesting.
- Identify your characters. Who are they? What do they look like? How do they act?
- Think about the setting. Where and when will your story take place?

Sam
- 13-year-old boy
- likes to keep up with older brother
- likes to snowboard
- takes risks
- brave
- determined

Paul
- 16-year-old boy
- encouraging/supportive
- likes to snowboard
- caring
- takes risks
- loyal
- thinks things through

≫ Step Two

- Identify the problem and the solution.

Problem	Solution
Sam and Paul were in an out-of-bounds area on the ski slopes and got caught in an avalanche.	They made it to safety and were found by the ski patrol team.

⟩➤ Step Three

- Plan your story. Think about the beginning, middle, and end.
  - The beginning sets the stage by introducing the characters, the setting, and the problem.
  - The middle describes how the characters deal with the problem.
  - The ending tells how the problem is solved.

⟩➤ Step Four

- Write your narrative.

  Keep these things in mind as you write your narrative:
  - Begin your story in an interesting way.
  - Bring your characters to life by using dialogue and describing their actions.
  - Show how characters react to events and to each other.
  - Use words, such as *first, then, after*, and *finally*, to show event order.
  - Use specific, concrete language to help put your readers in the middle of the story.

    walked ⟩   ambled⟩   strolled⟩   ran ⟩   sprinted⟩

- Wrap up your narrative.
  - What happened?
  - What did the characters learn?
  - What were the results?
  - Were there any consequences?

- Revise and edit your narrative before sharing.

Guide Notes

Title: **Out of Bounds**

Stage: Advanced Fluency

Text Form: Narrative

Approach: Guided Reading

Processes: Supporting Comprehension, Exploring Language, Processing Information

Writing Focus: Narrative

SUPPORTING COMPREHENSION

- Do you think Paul should have changed his plans when he knew Sam was going to follow him up the mountain? What reasons can you give to support your opinion?
- Look at pages 4–5. What inferences can you make about why the boys didn't see the warning signs?
- From what you know so far about the characters, do you think if they had seen the signs they would have gone on? Why or why not?
- Look at pages 6–7. What inferences can you make about Paul as a brother?
- Look at pages 8–9. Why do you think Sam wanted to show his brother he could handle the steep slope? Do you think he could justify the risk factor? Why or why not?
- Look at pages 12–13. What inferences can you make about how the boys reacted to the avalanche?
- Look at pages 14–15. What is meant by the phrase "the reality of the situation hit home"?
- Look at pages 16–17. How does author's use of the word "alive" take on a special significance in this context?
- Do you think the conclusion to this story is strong? Why or why not?
- Why do you think the author wrote this story?
- Who would you recommend this story to and why?

EXPLORING LANGUAGE

Vocabulary

Clarify: dodge, powder snow, gradually, out-of-bounds, painstakingly, pounding, thumbs up, compared to, burning desire, avalanche, headquarters, partially

Synonyms: Discuss synonyms for *warning, painstakingly, common*

Simile: *shaking like jelly, flew out like a wave behind his board*